Essential COOKING SERIES

COMPREHENSIVE, STEP-BY-STEP COOKING

Salads & Greens

HINKLER
BOOKS

D1444200

Essential Cooking Series: Salads & Greens
First published in 2009 by Hinkler Books Pty Ltd
45–55 Fairchild Street
Heatherton Victoria 3202 Australia
www.hinklerbooks.com

Disclaimer: The nutritional information listed under each recipe does not
include the nutrient content of garnishes or any accompaniments not listed
in specific quantitites in the ingredient list. The nutritional information for
each recipe is an estimate only, and may vary depending on the brand of
ingredients used, and due to natural biological variations in the composition
of natural foods such as meat, fish, fruit and vegetables. The nutritional
information was calculated by using Foodworks dietary analysis software
(Version 3, Xyris Software Pty Ltd, Highgate Hill, Queensland, Australia) based
on the Australian food composition tables and food manufacturers' data.
Where not specified, ingredients are always analysed as average or medium,
not small or large.

ISBN: 978 1 7418 5707 8

10 9 8 7 6 5 4 3 2
14 13 12 11 10

Printed and bound in China

Contents

An introduction to salads and greens

Crisp, refreshing, colourful, delicious, light, appealing, wholesome and healthy are all the words which come to mind when we think of salads. They are nature's gift to our health and to our meal table.

The value of salads in our diet cannot be underestimated. They provide, first and foremost, valuable nutrients such as vitamins and minerals, which are not lost through cooking. They add variety and interest to our diet, colour to our table and elevate the most simple meal.

Salad ingredients were once restricted to the traditional varieties of the various cuisines around the world. Today, with the interchange of ethnic cuisines, the demand for new salad produce has crossed continents and climatic zones and everything is available to all. We can all enjoy salad combinations outside our own traditional fare. We can combine the fruits of the tropics with the vegetables of the temperate zones, the flavours of the west with the more exotic flavours of the east. This book explores this amazing interchange.

Salads are not only for summer meals, they can and should be served all the year.

The following salad greens are known by several names. This guide will assist you to identify the ingredient you require.

Cos lettuce
Has a crisp leaf and a sweetish nutty flavour. Known as: cos, romaine.

Iceberg lettuce
Crisp leaves packed tightly into a round head. Known as: iceberg lettuce, crisphead lettuce.

Mignonette lettuce
Soft tender leaves tinged with red. Known as: mignonette lettuce, cabbage lettuce.

Green and red coral lettuce
Green or red frilled leaves. Do not form a heart. Known as: green coral or red coral, loose-leaf lettuce.

Butter lettuce
Tender soft-leaf lettuce with a buttery flavour. Known as: butter lettuce, butterhead.

Endive
Crisp leaf with a slight bitter flavour. Known as: endive, chicory, curly endive.

Rocket
A flavoursome leaf with a mustard tang. Known as: rocket, roquette, arugula.

Radicchio
A beautiful ruby colour with thick white veins; a very attractive leaf for presentation. Known as: radicchio, red-leaved chicory, Italian chicory, Italian red lettuce.

Witlof
Crisp white leaves with a mild bitter flavour. Known as: witlof, Belgian endive, French endive, witlof chicory.

Spring onions
A young bulb onion harvested before the bulb has formed. With a mild flavour and crisp texture, it is in great demand for salads. Known as: green onions, spring onions, scallions, Welsh onions, bunching onions.

Red onions
Red in colour, these onions have a mild sweetish flavour. There are many varieties. Known as: Italian red onion, Spanish onion.

Flat-leaf parsley
Parsley with a flat leaf and a more intense flavour than the curly parsley. Known as: flat-leaf parsley, continental parsley.

Salad tips and skills

Salad greens and other salad vegetables must be stored correctly to retain freshness and quality. Do not wash any vegetables before storing. Greens that are tied in bunches, such as spinach, endive and rocket, should be opened out and checked. If damp in the centre, pat dry before storing.

Salad greens should be stored in the vegetable compartment of the refrigerator. As the level of vegetables in the compartment lowers, place a clean kitchen towel lightly over their surface to prevent moisture being drawn from them to fill the space. Have you ever wondered why the last few pieces in the vegetable compartment have wilted?

If there is no room in the vegetable container, salad vegetables may be placed on the lower shelves in a plastic bag, covered plastic container or on a tray covered with a clean cloth or plastic wrap. The important point is to cover their surface to prevent moisture loss.

Root vegetables may be stored on a rack in a well-ventilated dark place.

All vegetables and fruits must be washed well before peeling and cutting. Salad greens must be washed well in 2–3 changes of water to remove all grit, or in a colander under trickling cold water, to avoid bruising the tender leaves. Drain well.

Root vegetables need to be scrubbed with a brush under running water to remove all dirt, particularly if cooked with the skin on.

For a good salad, leaves need to be dried well before placing in the bowl. The dressing will not adhere to wet leaves and the excess moisture will dilute the dressing. A salad spinner is excellent. It will spin all the water off. You may also pat dry the leaves with absorbent paper or shake dry in a clean kitchen cloth.

To crisp the salad leaves, roll up in a damp cloth and refrigerate for 1 hour or until you are ready to serve.

Deseeding tomatoes

Cut the tomato in half across the centre. Cup the tomato in your hand and squeeze out the seeds.

To trim asparagus

Using a potato peeler or sharp paring knife, peel off the thicker skin on the lower part of the stalk.

To segment an orange or grapefruit

1 Peel the orange or grapefruit thickly, removing all the white pith.

2 Holding the orange or grapefruit over a bowl to catch the juice, cut close to the membrane on each side of the segment and ease the segment out. Continue to the next segment.

To deseed a cucumber

Cut the cucumber in half lengthwise. Run the point of a teaspoon down the seeds, pressing inwards to remove the seeds.

To toast nuts

Place nuts on a shallow oven tray and place in a moderate oven – 180°C (350°F, gas mark 4) – for 10 minutes or until golden. The nuts will crisp on cooling. A deep colouration will impart a bitter flavour.

OR

Heat a heavy-based frying pan until hot. Add the nuts and stir with a wooden spoon until they colour. Remove from the pan as soon as desired colour is attained.

To blanch almonds

Place in a bowl and cover with hot water. Stand for 10 minutes, then slip off skins.

To peel capsicum (pepper)

Trim the top and base of each capsicum (pepper) and cut into quarters, making 4 flat pieces. Trim off any inside veins

and rub skin side with oil. Place skin-side up under a preheated hot grill and cook until skins are blistered. Place in a plastic bag, closing the end, and set aside until cool enough to handle. With the aid of a small knife, lift the edge of the skin and peel off.

Tuscan tomato and bean salad

INGREDIENTS

12 sun-dried tomato halves
1 cup (250 ml, 8 fl oz) boiling water
$^1/_3$ cup (80 ml, 2$^3/_4$ floz) rice vinegar
1 tablespoon olive oil
2 teaspoons honey
salt and pepper to taste
150 g (5 oz) watercress
150 g (5 oz) baby rocket leaves
8 roma tomatoes, diced
6 spring onions
  (green onions), sliced
80 g (2$^3/_4$ oz) kalamata olives,
  stones removed
2 x 440 g (14 oz) cans cannellini beans,
  rinsed and drained
100 g (3$^1/_2$ oz) toasted walnuts, chopped
serves 4–6

PREPARATION TIME
15 minutes

1 Soak the sun-dried tomatoes in the boiling water until water cools. Place sun-dried tomatoes and water in a food processor. Add the rice vinegar, oil and honey and purée until smooth. Add salt and pepper to taste.

2 Pluck the watercress sprigs from the coarse stems, and thoroughly wash with the rocket. Drain well and shake dry in a clean towel. Place in a large mixing bowl and add the diced tomatoes, spring onions (green onions), olives and cannellini beans.

3 Pour the sun-dried tomato dressing over the salad and toss well to coat. Serve immediately, garnished with the toasted walnuts.

| NUTRITIONAL VALUE PER SERVE | FAT 3.4 G | CARBOHYDRATE 7.1 G | PROTEIN 3.9 G |

Dressing: a mixture added to completed dishes to add moisture and flavour, eg salads, cooked vegetables.

Drizzle: to pour in a fine thread-like stream moving over a surface.

Egg wash: beaten egg with milk or water used to brush over pastry, bread dough or biscuits to give a sheen and golden brown colour.

Essence: a strong flavouring liquid, usually made by distillation. Only a few drops are needed to flavour.

Fillet: a piece of prime meat, fish or poultry which is boneless or has all bones removed.

Flake: to separate cooked fish into flakes, removing any bones and skin, using 2 forks.

Flame: to ignite warmed alcohol over food or to pour into a pan with food, ignite, then serve.

Flute: to make decorative indentations around the pastry rim before baking.

Fold in: combining of a light, whisked or creamed mixture with other ingredients. Add a portion of the other ingredients at a time and mix using a gentle circular motion, over and under the mixture so that air will not be lost. Use a metal spoon or spatula.

Glaze: to brush or coat food with a liquid that will give the finished product a glossy appearance, and on baked products, a golden brown colour.

Grease: to rub the surface of a metal or heatproof dish with oil or fat, to prevent the food from sticking.

Herbed butter: softened butter mixed with finely chopped fresh herbs and re-chilled. Used to serve on grilled meats and fish.

Hors d'oeuvre: small savoury foods served as an appetiser, popularly known today as 'finger food'.

Infuse: to steep foods in a liquid until the liquid absorbs their flavour.

Joint: to cut poultry and game into serving pieces by dividing at the joint.

Julienne: to cut some food, eg vegetables and processed meats, into fine strips the length of matchsticks. Used in salads or as a garnish to cooked dishes.

Knead: to work a yeast dough in a pressing, stretching and folding motion with the heel of the hand until smooth and elastic to develop the gluten strands. Non-yeast doughs should be lightly and quickly handled as gluten development is not desired.

Line: to cover the inside of a baking tin with paper for the easy removal of the cooked product from the baking tin.

Macerate: to stand fruit in a syrup, liqueur or spirit to give added flavour.

Marinade: a flavoured liquid, into which food is placed for some time to give it flavour and to tenderise. Marinades include an acid ingredient such as vinegar or wine, oil and seasonings.

Mask: to evenly cover cooked food portions with a sauce, mayonnaise or savoury jelly.

Pan-fry: to fry foods in a small amount of fat or oil, sufficient to coat the base of the pan.

Parboil: to boil until partially cooked. The food is then finished by some other method.

Pare: to peel the skin from vegetables and fruit. 'Peel' is the popular term but 'pare' is the name given to the knife used; paring knife.

Pit: to remove stones or seeds from olives, cherries, dates.

Pith: the white lining between the rind and flesh of oranges, grapefruit and lemons.

Pitted: the olives, cherries, dates etc. with the stone removed, eg purchase pitted dates.

Poach: to simmer gently in enough hot liquid to almost cover the food so its shape will be retained.

Pound: to flatten meats with a meat mallet; to reduce to a paste or small particles with a mortar and pestle.

Simmer: to cook in liquid just below boiling point at about 96°C (205°F) with small bubbles rising gently to the surface.

Skim: to remove fat or froth from the surface of simmering food.

Stock: the liquid produced when meat, poultry, fish or vegetables have been simmered in water to extract the flavour. Used as a base for soups, sauces, casseroles etc. Convenience stock products are available.

Sweat: to cook sliced onions or vegetables in a small amount of butter in a covered pan over low heat, to soften them and release flavour without colouring.

Conversions

Measurements differ from country to country, so it's important to understand what the differences are. This Measurements Guide gives you simple 'at-a-glance' information for using the recipes in this book, wherever you may be.

Cooking is not an exact science – minor variations in measurements won't make a difference to your cooking.

EQUIPMENT

There is a difference in the size of measuring cups used internationally, but the difference is minimal (only 2–3 teaspoons). We use the Australian standard metric measurements in our recipes:

1 teaspoon.....5 ml   1 tablespoon.....20 ml
1/2 cup.....125 ml   1 cup.....250 ml
4 cups.....1 litre

Measuring cups come in sets of one cup (250 ml), 1/2 cup (125 ml), 1/3 cup (80 ml) and 1/4 cup (60 ml). Use these for measuring liquids and certain dry ingredients.

Measuring spoons come in a set of four and should be used for measuring dry and liquid ingredients.

When using cup or spoon measures, always make them level (unless the recipe indicates otherwise).

DRY VERSUS WET INGREDIENTS

While this system of measures is consistent for liquids, it's more difficult to quantify dry ingredients. For instance, one level cup equals: 200 g of brown sugar; 210 g of caster sugar; and 110 g of icing sugar.

When measuring dry ingredients such as flour, don't push the flour down or shake it into the cup. It is best just to spoon the flour in until it reaches the desired amount. When measuring liquids, use a clear vessel indicating metric levels.

Always use medium eggs (55–60 g) when eggs are required in a recipe.

OVEN

Your oven should always be at the right temperature before placing the food in it to be cooked. Note that if your oven doesn't have a fan you may need to cook food for a little longer.

MICROWAVE

It is difficult to give an exact cooking time for microwave cooking. It is best to watch what you are cooking closely to monitor its progress.

STANDING TIME

Many foods continue to cook when you take them out of the oven or microwave. If a recipe states that the food needs to 'stand' after cooking, be sure not to overcook the dish.

CAN SIZES

The can sizes available in your supermarket or grocery store may not be the same as specified in the recipe. Don't worry if there is a small variation in size – it's unlikely to make a difference to the end result.

dry		liquids	
metric (grams)	imperial (ounces)	metric (millilitres)	imperial (fluid ounces)
		30 ml	1 fl oz
30 g	1 oz	60 ml	2 fl oz
60 g	2 oz	90 ml	3 fl oz
90 g	3 oz	100 ml	3 $\frac{1}{2}$ fl oz
100 g	3 $\frac{1}{2}$ oz	125 ml	4 fl oz
125 g	4 oz	150 ml	5 fl oz
150 g	5 oz	190 ml	6 fl oz
185 g	6 oz	250 ml	8 fl oz
200 g	7 oz	300 ml	10 fl oz
250 g	8 oz	500 ml	16 fl oz
280 g	9 oz	600 ml	20 fl oz (1 pint)*
315 g	10 oz	1000 ml (1 litre)	32 fl oz
330 g	11 oz		
370 g	12 oz		
400 g	13 oz		
440 g	14 oz		
470 g	15 oz		
500 g	16 oz (1 lb)		
750 g	24 oz (1 $\frac{1}{2}$ lb)		
1000 g (1 kg)	32 oz (2 lb)		*Note: an American pint is 16 fl oz.

cooking temperatures	°C (celsius)	°F (fahrenheit)	gas mark
very slow	120	250	$\frac{1}{2}$
slow	150	300	2
moderately slow	160	315	2–3
moderate	180	350	4
moderately hot	190	375	5
	200	400	6
hot	220	425	7
very hot	230	450	8
	240	475	9
	250	500	10

Index

Essential COOKING SERIES

COMPREHENSIVE, STEP-BY-STEP COOKING

Essential COOKING SERIES
COMPREHENSIVE, STEP-BY-STEP COOKING

Baking

Essential COOKING SERIES
COMPREHENSIVE, STEP-BY-STEP COOKING

Chicken Meals

Essential COOKING SERIES
COMPREHENSIVE, STEP-BY-STEP COOKING

Salads & Greens

Essential COOKING SERIES
COMPREHENSIVE, STEP-BY-STEP COOKING

Soups & Hors D'Oeuvres

Essential COOKING SERIES
COMPREHENSIVE, STEP-BY-STEP COOKING

Meat Dishes

Essential COOKING SERIES
COMPREHENSIVE, STEP-BY-STEP COOKING

Finger Food

Essential COOKING SERIES
COMPREHENSIVE, STEP-BY-STEP COOKING

Pasta Dishes

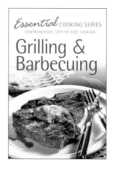

Essential COOKING SERIES
COMPREHENSIVE, STEP-BY-STEP COOKING

Grilling & Barbecuing

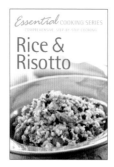

Essential COOKING SERIES
COMPREHENSIVE, STEP-BY-STEP COOKING

Rice & Risotto

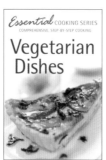

Essential COOKING SERIES
COMPREHENSIVE, STEP-BY-STEP COOKING

Vegetarian Dishes

Essential COOKING SERIES
COMPREHENSIVE, STEP-BY-STEP COOKING

Asian Dishes

Essential COOKING SERIES
COMPREHENSIVE, STEP-BY-STEP COOKING

Stir-Fry